DISCOVERING
Little
Things

G/L Regal Venture Books
A Division of G/L Publications
Glendale, California, USA

557

In the world God made
even the little things
are beautiful.

Hold up your finger and look at it closely.
It is marked with a pattern of lines.
God made the pattern
on each person's fingers
different from all others.
No one else in all the world has yours.
It is your special fingerprint design.

4

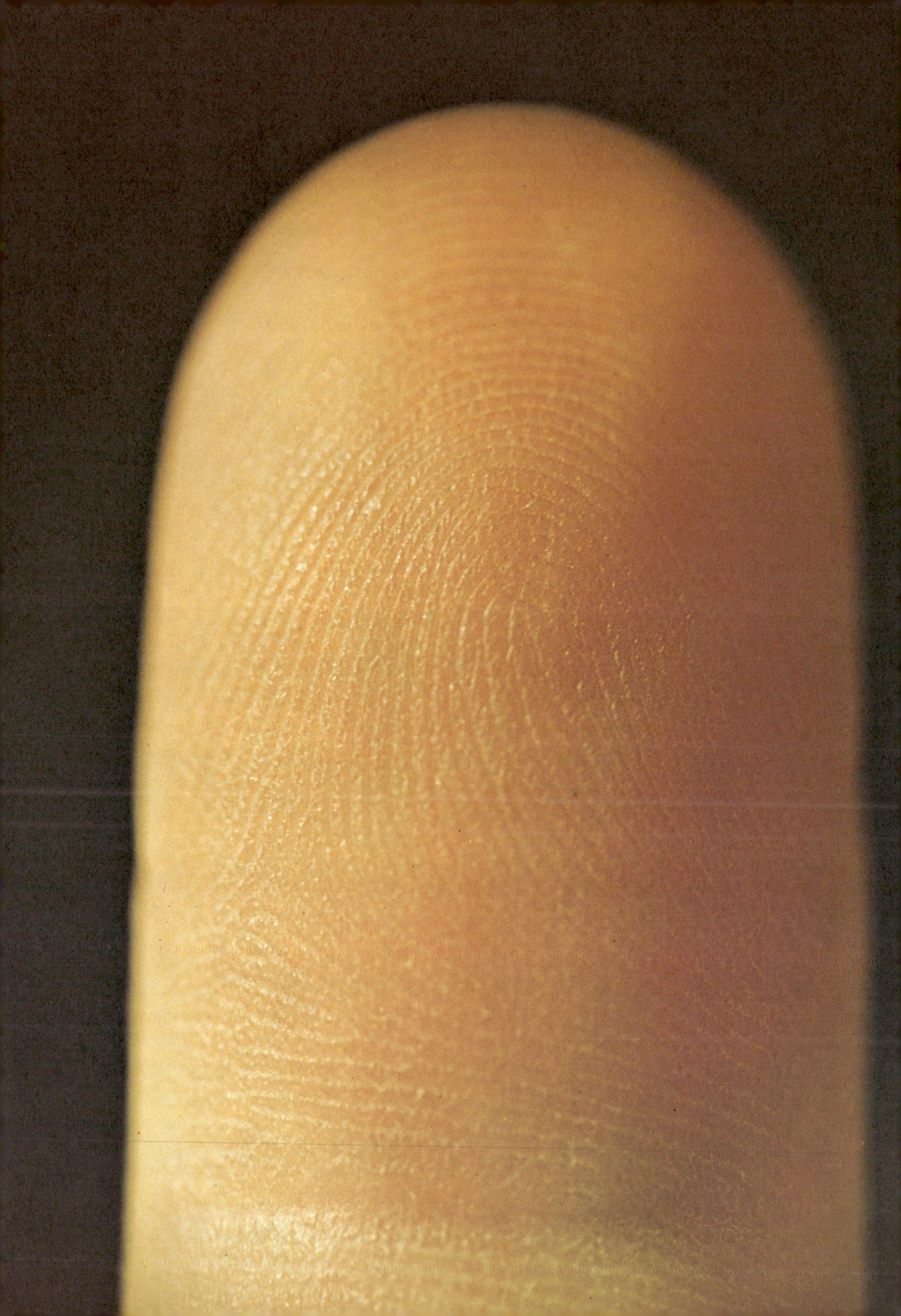

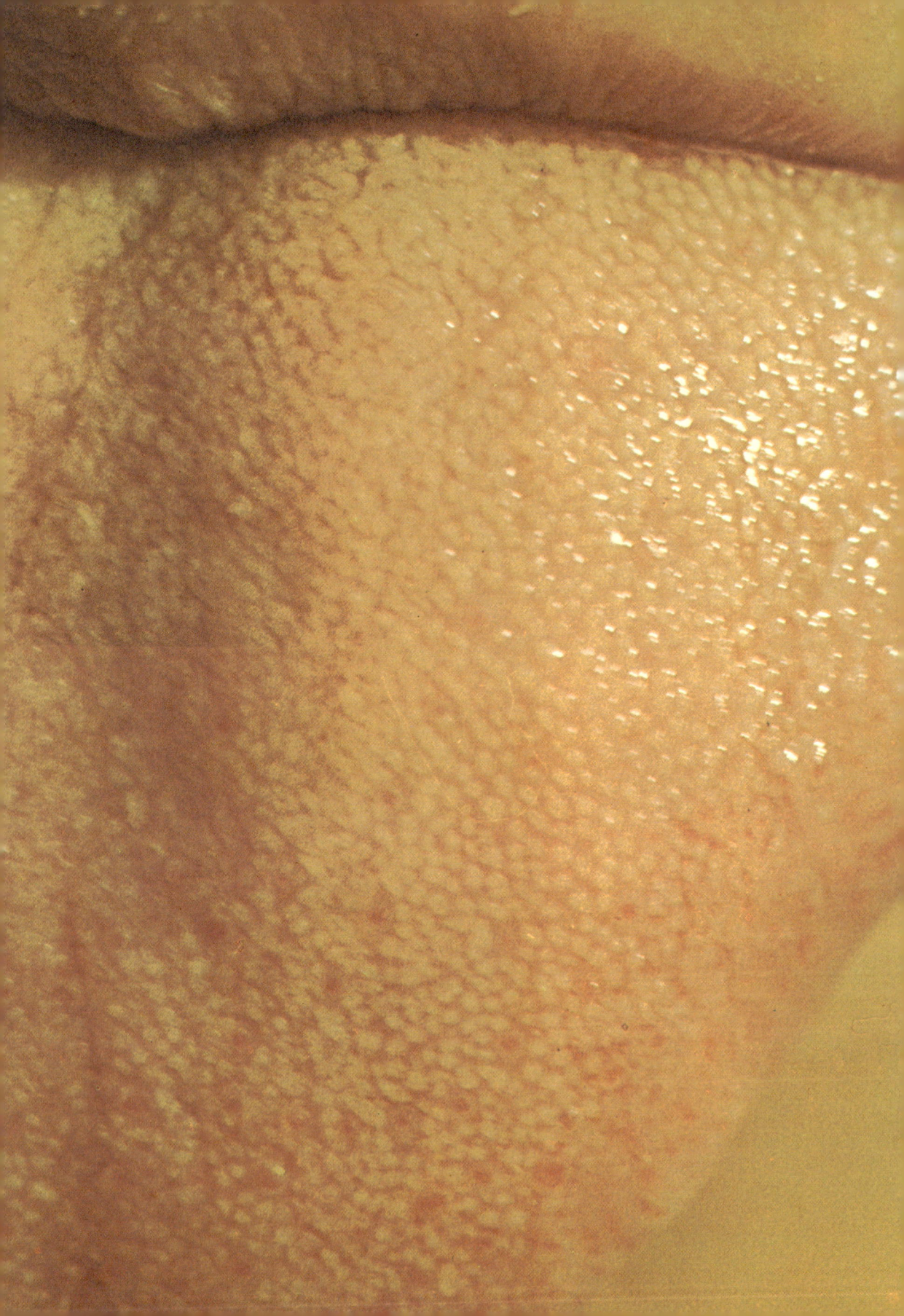

Here is a funny thing. It's all lumps and bumps. What do you think it is?

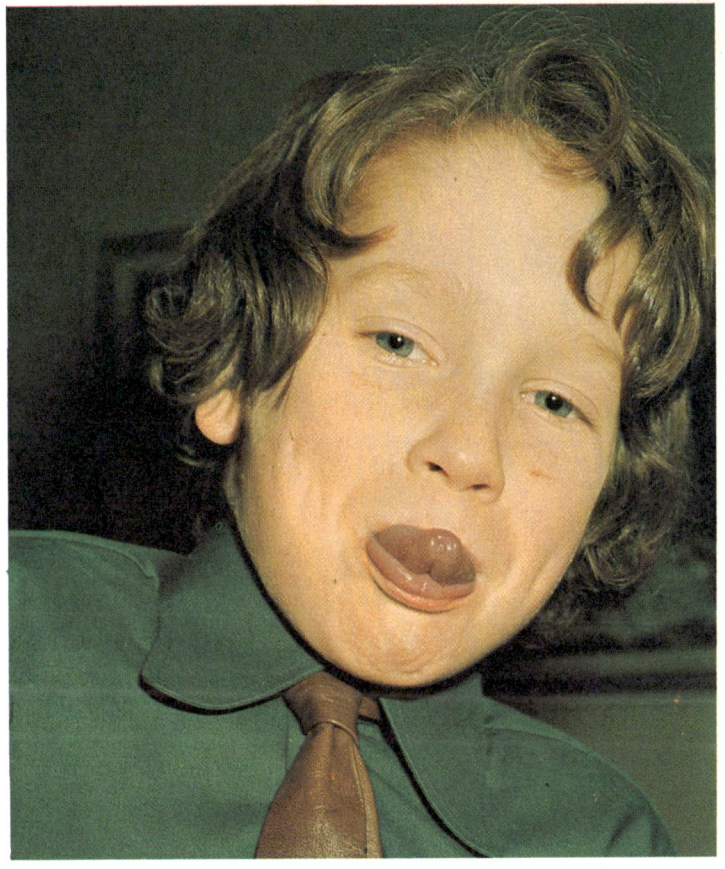

It's the end of your tongue!
Look at your tongue in the mirror.
Do you see the tiny bumps?
God made the bumps to help you taste things.

God made this butterfly's wings
of little scales, like feathers.
They all fit together like this.

Each one is in the right place
to make up the beautiful colors we see.
If you touch a butterfly's wing,
the scales come off on your fingers like
fine dust. Then he may not be able to fly.

Did you ever wonder
why God made long whiskers
on a rabbit's nose?
A rabbit feels things with his whiskers
rather like we do with our fingers.
10

Does this look like yellow grass?
It's a field of yellow flowers.
Can you count them? God made
each flower to look like this one.

Just think
how many flowers there must be
in this one field!

Did you know God made a feather
to hold together with hooks,
thousands of them on each
feather frond.

Find a feather.
Look at it closely.
If you pull the fronds apart,
you will feel the tiny hooks gripping.

This is a dragonfly. You can see him
flying around in the summertime.
If you could get close enough
you would see that he has great big eyes.

God made each eye in patterns like this.

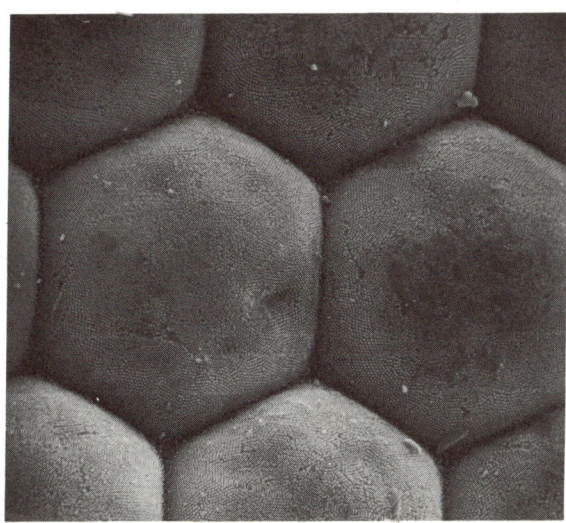

From the outside,
most stones look very ordinary.
Ask someone to break one in half for you.
Then wet the pieces of stone.
You will see that God has hidden
some beautiful colors inside.

Have you ever seen little round eggs
like this one on a leaf?
They may have been laid
by a butterfly or moth.

Each egg has a different pattern,
like this moth's egg.

God made leaves in many shapes and sizes.
When you look closely at a leaf,
you can see a pattern made by its veins.
In spring and summer
most leaves are green.
In autumn they turn brown and gold.
How many shapes and colors can you find?

This is a bee visiting a flower.
Can you see the pollen from the flower
like dust on his back legs?
Close up, each speck of pollen dust
has a lovely pattern like this.

The pollen dust from each flower
makes a different pattern.

If you look very closely
at just one drop of pond water,
you can see thousands
of tiny plants and animals.

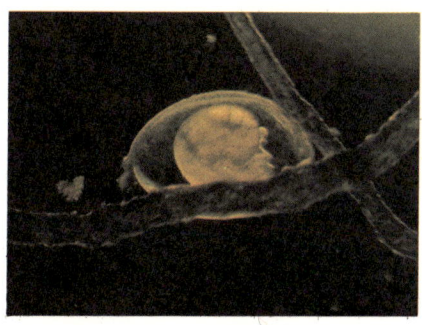

This is a snail's egg
in a drop
of pond water.
You can see right
through it.

This is a tiny crab.

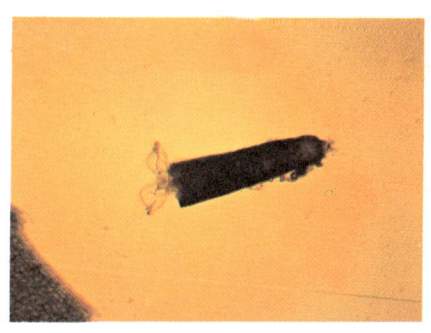

This animal lives
in a tube.
He moves about by
wiggling the paddles
you can see
in the picture.

God has made such a wonderful world
full of patterns and colors.
He has given us eyes
to see and enjoy them.
Look around carefully.
You can discover more of God's wonders
for yourself.

"For the Lord God created the heavens
and earth, and put everything in
place, and he made the world to be
lived in." Isaiah 45:18